Gluten-Free Baking

Perfect Gluten Free Bread, Cookies, Cakes, Muffins and other Gluten Intolerance Recipes for Healthy Eating on a Gluten-Free Diet

The Essential Cookbook for Beginners to Avoid Celiac Disease

Tiffany Shelton

Disclaimer

The recipes and information in this book are provided for educational purposes only. Please always consult a licensed professional before making changes to your lifestyle or diet. The author and publisher shall have neither liability nor responsibility to anyone with respect to any loss or damage caused or alleged to be caused directly or indirectly by the information contained in this book. All trademarks and brands within this book are for clarifying purposes only and are owned by the owners themselves, not affiliated with this document.

Images from shutterstock.com

CONTENTS

INTRODUCTION

According to the National Institute of Health in the US, around 1 in every 133 Americans may be affected by celiac disease, but 97 percent of sufferers will go undiagnosed. It's also estimated that between 5 and 10 percent of the world's population may be suffering some form of gluten sensitivity. A growing number of doctors believe gluten consumption is directly responsible for many common intestinal and nonintestinal complaints, and symptoms can be improved greatly or completely cured by removing gluten from the diet.

Living gluten-free doesn't mean you have to sacrifice your favorite baked goods. In fact, each of the more than 55 easy-to-make recipes found in this book is the result of passion to take the everyday comfort foods we each hold dear and reinvent them so that they're not only acceptable gluten-free substitutes for old favorites, but are so delightfully flavorful that you won't even notice anything is missing.

Baking is an art as well as a science. My heartfelt mission in writing this book is to provide you with a whole host of deliciously comforting gluten-free baking recipes, while also inspiring you to rediscover the joy of sharing your delightful creations with those you love. With the easy, delicious recipes found in this book, your kitchen can once again become a welcome gathering place for you, your family, and friends to break bread and share your lives with one another.

CHAPTER 1. The Basics

What is Gluten?

Gluten is an elastic substance found in grains such as wheat, barley and rye. It is nearly everywhere, most especially in processed food items. It is found in almost every product from cereal to salad dressings.

You can see below on how gluten can end up on foodstuffs we purchase:

- Wheat is found in baked products, soups, breads and pasta
- Barley is found in food coloring, malt vinegar, beer
- Rye is found in rye bread, rye beer and cereals

Gluten is a concern because it is associated with several medical conditions. Gluten itself has absolutely no nutritional or health-promoting value—our bodies have no use for it. Sugar, which also faces similar loathing, has some nutritional value as a source of energy. There is no medical information or study concluding that consumption of gluten can promote good health.

Instead, gluten causes disease. Humans have varying degrees of intolerance to gluten, some may feel no symptoms at all while others experience full-blown symptoms of gluten intolerance. Our bodies actually view gluten as a foreign non-food substance. Gluten provokes the immune system to respond pathologically and result to disease. This same thing happens in the condition celiac disease.

Gluten in our food makes us sick and we must do something to get it out of our life. You will find this book very useful in adopting a gluten-free lifestyle.

The most common symptoms of gluten intolerance are:

- Unexplained fatigue
- Gastrointestinal distress (gas, bloating, diarrhea, constipation, vomiting, reflux)
- Headaches (including migraines)
- Mouth sores
- Unintended weight loss/gain
- Inability to concentrate
- Moodiness/depression
- Amenorrhea/delayed menarche (menstrual cycles)
- Bone/joint/muscle pain
- Tingling numbness in the legs
- Thinning of scalp hair
- Anemia
- Chronic abdominal pain

Celiac disease or gluten intolerance worsens symptoms of the following conditions:

- Crohn's disease
- Dermatitis herpetiformis (a "sister" of celiac disease)
- Down syndrome
- Epilepsy
- Gall bladder disease
- Hyperthyroidism/hypothyroidism
- Total IgA deficiency
- Insulin-dependent diabetes (Type 1)
- Infertility
- IBS (Irritable Bowel Syndrome)
- Malnutrition
- Multiple sclerosis
- Non-Hodgkin's lymphoma
- Osteoporosis, osteopenia, osteomalacia
- Pancreatic disorders
- Bone fractures
- Peripheral neuropathy
- Primary biliary cirrhosis
- Psoriasis
- Recurrent stomatitis
- Rheumatoid arthritis

- Sclerosing cholangitis
- Sjogren syndrome
- Systemic lupus

- Turner syndrome
- Ulcerative colitis
- Vitiligo

Many people are not aware that they become sicker due to consumption of gluten. Eliminating gluten is an important factor for disease recovery and optimal health.

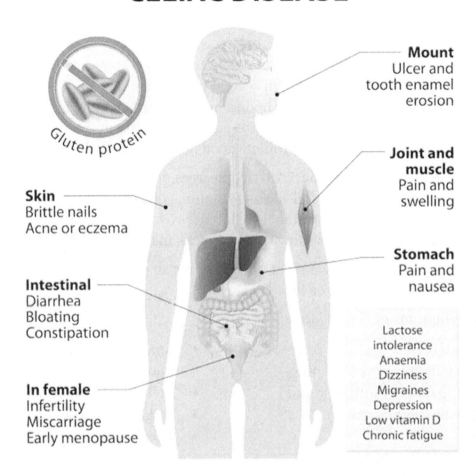

CELIAC DISEASE

Mount
Ulcer and tooth enamel erosion

Joint and muscle
Pain and swelling

Stomach
Pain and nausea

Skin
Brittle nails
Acne or eczema

Intestinal
Diarrhea
Bloating
Constipation

In female
Infertility
Miscarriage
Early menopause

Gluten protein

Lactose intolerance
Anaemia
Dizziness
Migraines
Depression
Low vitamin D
Chronic fatigue

Managing a Gluten-free Diet

Whilst it is easy to avoid products that obviously contain wheat and gluten—bread, cakes, pasta—there are a variety of products that contain traces of gluten, some of which are not obvious. It is not always easy to avoid such pitfalls and it is therefore essential to carefully check the ingredients list on product packaging or refer to the manufacturer to ensure that products are gluten-free. At the outset of a gluten-free diet, you want to keep a food diary to record what you eat, as this can help identify problem foods that have made you ill.

All forms of wheat, barley, rye, and spelt must be avoided. This means that regular flours and breads are out, as well as wheat-based products such as beer and pasta. Gluten is also commonly used by food manufacturers in a wide variety of food preparation and can be found in ready-meals and pre-produced food. Wheat used as a thickener in a sauce or products coated in breadcrumbs are also not suitable for people with gluten intolerance.

You need to be extra vigilant at all stages of cooking. It is so easy to take a packet from the kitchen cupboard and add it to a recipe without checking whether the item contains gluten—I have found myself doing this on occasion and have just stopped myself in time. I once made stock from chicken bones of a roast chicken, but the chicken had contained a breadcrumb stuffing so there was a good chance that the stock was contaminated with gluten. Luckily, I remembered in time before serving it to my friend who has celiac disease. With time and practice, you will become familiar with which ingredients are safe and which are not. The best advice is just to take a bit of time before you start cooking. Assemble all of your ingredients and check that they are all safe to use before starting to cook.

Some of the less obvious products that contain gluten include:

Anti-caking agents – these are used to prevent clumping and sticking together of ingredients during food production and can contain traces of wheat. Anticaking agents are commonly found in some icing/confectioner sugars and dried fruits. When using these sugars and dried fruits, always check the labels carefully to ensure that they do not contain an anti-caking agent. Powdered fondant icing sugar (which contains glucose) and unrefined icing/confectioner sugar do not generally contain an anti-caking agent and can be used to make glacé, royal and butter icings/frostings successfully. When selecting dried fruit, choose brands use a light coating of oil rather than an anti-caking agent.

Yeast – some dried yeasts contain wheat as a bulking agent. For safe gluten-free baking, use either fresh yeast or a gluten-free dried yeast, both of which are stocked by most supermarkets and health food shops.

Baking powder – some baking powders contain wheat. Many manufacturers are now using rice flour in place of wheat flour and so gluten-free baking powder is now more commonly available in supermarkets.

Dried milk powder/non-fat dry milk – some milk powders/non-fat dry milk are bulked out with wheat. In addition, some celiacs cannot tolerate white or milk chocolate because lactose intolerance is associated with celiac disease, although it is a temporary condition in the vast majority of people that rectifies itself after a person establishes themselves on a gluten-free diet.

Malt products – malted drinks should all be avoided as they are wheat based, but malt extract can usually be tolerated in small amounts, e.g. in breakfast cereals. Malt vinegar is suitable as the protein is removed in the processing.

Soy sauce and Worcestershire sauce – these also contain gluten so look out for gluten-free brands.

Processed meat products – products such as sausages, salamis and pâtés can contain traces of wheat so always read the labels carefully.

Sauces, gravy powders, stocks (cubes and liquid) and powdered spices – these can sometimes be bulked out with wheat products so again always check the labels carefully.

Instant coffees – some contain wheat as a bulking agent. Fresh ground coffee, which can be used to make espresso or filter coffee in a machine can be used instead as these generally do not contain any gluten.

Glacé cherries – use fresh cherries or preserved cherries as a good substitute in baking; plus, they always taste nicer.

Sour cream – some processes for making sour cream use wheat, so it is important to use a brand that is gluten-free. Checking the manufacturer's website will assist with this.

The above list is not exhaustive but should give you a good idea of just how rigorous you have to be with product checking when you are cooking for someone with a gluten intolerance.

Baking Basics

Cooking is a form of art, but science is also part of the equation. While savory recipes are tolerant of virtually endless substitutions, baked goods are not. Each ingredient performs a specific function in a recipe based on a certain quantity to create a batter or dough. These are general pointers on procedures to be used for all types of baked goods

✓ Measure accurately

Measure dry ingredients in dry measuring cups, which are plastic or metal, and come in sizes of 1/4, 1/3, 1/2, and 1 cup. Spoon dry ingredients from the container or canister into the measuring cup, and then sweep the top with a straight edge such as the back of a knife or a spatula to measure it properly. Do not dip the cup into the canister or tap it on the counter to produce a level surface. These methods pack down the dry ingredients and can increase the actual volume by up to 10 percent. Tablespoons and teaspoons should also be leveled; a rounded 1/2 tsp can really measure almost 1 tsp. If the box or can does not have a straight edge built in, level the excess in the spoon back into the container with the back of a knife blade. Measure liquids in liquid measures, which come in different sizes but are transparent glass or plastic and have lines on the sides. To accurately measure liquids, place the measuring cup on a flat counter and bend down to read the marked level.

✓ Create consistent temperature

All ingredients should be at room temperature unless otherwise indicated. Having all ingredients at the same temperature makes it easier to combine them into a smooth, homogeneous mixture. Adding cold liquid to a dough or batter can cause the batter to lose its unified structure by making the fat rigid.

✓ Preheat the oven

Some ovens can take up to 25 minutes to reach a high temperature such as 450°F. The minimum heating time should be 15 minutes.

✓ Plan ahead

Read the recipe thoroughly and assemble all your ingredients. Account for all ingredients required for a recipe in advance, so you don't get to a step and realize you must improvise. Assembling in advance also lessens the risk of over-mixing dough or batters as the mixer drones on while you search for a specific spice.

✓ Careful creaming

Perhaps the most vital step in the creation of a cake batter is the creaming of the butter and sugar. During this process, air is beaten in and is trapped in the butter's crystalline structure. It is the number and size of the air bubbles (which then become enlarged by the carbon dioxide produced by baking soda or baking powder) that leavens a dough or batter to produce a high, finely-textured product.

The starting point in proper creaming is to ensure that the butter is at the correct temperature, approximately 70°F. Remove butter from the refrigerator and cut each stick into approximately 30 slices. Allow them to sit at room temperature for 15-20 minutes to soften.

Begin creaming by beating the butter alone in a mixer until it has broken into small pieces. Then add the sugar and beat at medium speed to start the process of combining them. Then increase the speed to high, and scrape the bowl frequently. When properly creamed, the texture of the butter and sugar mixture will be light and fluffy.

Important Equipment

There is very little specialized equipment needed for baking the recipes in this book. You'll need a selection of baking pans for the cakes and tortes in Chapter 2, a few pie plates, and some cookie sheets. Here is a list of the machines and gadgets I used developing the recipes for this book:

- **Microplane grater**

These resemble a flat kitchen spatula but with tiny holes in it. They're fabulous for grating citrus zest and fibrous foods such as ginger or nutmeg, and you can also use them for Parmesan cheese and even garlic cloves for other recipes.

- **Food processor**

The base needs to be cleaned thoroughly before making any gluten-free item, but for very little money you can purchase a second work bowl. The work bowl of food processors is made of plastic that can harbor food particles once scratched.

- **Wire cooling racks**

Wire cooling racks are essential, and there's really no substitute for them. The type of rack on top of a broiler pan is too solid, and there's nothing that makes baked goods lose their texture—especially those made with gluten-free ingredients—faster than placing them on an impervious surface.

- **A powerful mixer**

Some of these bread doughs are very thick, and a standard mixer that sits on the counter is the best friend you can have. While hand-held mixers are fine for small tasks, the stand mixer is what is best for baking. The paddle attachment makes the thickest substance look easy to blend, and the dough hook takes all the labor out of kneading.

- **Offset spatulas**

An offset spatula is the type of spatula with the handle raised up from the level of the blade to make transferring cookies from the baking sheets to the cooling racks comfortable.

The Gluten-free Baking Pantry

For successful baking, you need to equip yourself with a few basic ingredients. Once you have developed confidence from following these recipes, you can then experiment with other recipes. Below is a list of essential ingredients you will need for baking the recipes from this book.

Gluten-free blended flours – there are ready mixed and specifically designed to give the best results. Whilst you can combine your own mixes of rice, potato and corn flour/cornstarch, it is more convenient to use these ready-mixed flours.

Buckwheat flour – contrary to its name, buckwheat does not contain any wheat at all. It is made from the seeds of a flowering plant that is associated with the rhubarb family. The seeds look similar to beechnuts and it is a common misunderstanding that this flour is made from beechnuts. The flour has a strong taste, which can be quite overpowering and slightly medicinal if used in large quantities. This flour is ideal for pancakes and blinis and can be used in some cakes. Be aware that a very small number of people experience an allergic reaction to buckwheat so it's always essential to check with the person you are baking for.

Chestnut flour – this is made from ground sweet chestnuts and has a delicious smoky flavor. Due to this smokiness, however, it is only really suitable for savory recipes.

Gram flour – this is made from ground chickpeas and is often used in Indian cookery. It can be used to make pakora and bhajis and also various Indian flatbreads. Most poppadoms are made with gram flour but it is important to check that it has not been combined with wheat flour. Italian Farina di Ceci is a similar product and can be substituted.

Coconut flour – this is made from dried coconut flesh which has been ground to a fine powder. You can make your own by grinding desiccated coconut to a fine powder in a food processor and then sifting it, although if your desiccated coconut is sweetened you will need to reduce the sugar in the recipe and check that the desiccated coconut does not contain any wheat as an anti-caking agent or coating.

Cornflour/cornstarch – this is made from finely ground grains of corn. It is an excellent thickener and can be used in sauces.

Polenta/cornmeal – this is a useful staple of gluten-free baking. Coarse grains can be cooked in water to a thick paste and added to cakes and breads to give a lovely golden color, moist texture and rich flavor. Fine meal is more like flour in texture and can be used in breads and muffins.

Almond meal and ground almonds – almond meal is a coarse ground flour which contains the skin of the whole almonds. It is therefore darker in texture than ground almonds and is ideal in cookies and cakes. Ground almonds are one of the most common ingredients in this book as they make cakes very moist and do not have a strong flavor so can carry other flavors well. You can make your own ground almonds or almond meal by blitzing whole or skinned almonds in a food processor. When buying ready ground almonds, check the ingredients, as some cheap varieties include breadcrumbs, and therefore gluten, as a bulking agent.

Nuts – a lot of the recipes in this book use other ground nuts, such as pecans, walnuts and hazelnuts. They are an ideal replacement for flour as they create a moist texture and add delicious flavor. If you do not have the nut called for in the recipe, you can generally substitute another nut in its place. By grinding the nuts in a food processor until very fine then combining them with a small amount of gluten-free flour they make an ideal substitute.

Gluten-free baking powder – this is an essential raising/rising agent and is used to make cakes and breads rise during baking.

Xanthan gum – this is used in gluten-free baking to bind, thicken and stabilize ingredients and is ideal for use in doughs, pastry and breads. It's made by fermenting corn sugar with a microbial bacteria and is used extensively in the food industry.

Extra virgin coconut oil – this is usually sold in jars in a set form and adds a delicious coconut flavor to recipes.

Flavoring agents – vanilla and almond extracts are ideal for masking the sometimes mildly unpleasant flavor of gluten-free flours. Always check the labeling to ensure that flavorings are gluten-free.

Dairy ingredients – these are essential for moist, non-crumbly cakes. In this book, the recipes use buttermilk, plain yogurt and sour cream. Again, it is essential to check the product labels as some creams may contain traces of gluten. If you prefer, you can make your own sour cream by adding the juice of a lemon to 300 ml/1¼ cups double/heavy cream. If you do not have the liquid ingredient called for in the recipe, you can easily substitute. For example, if you do not have buttermilk available, mix together half milk and half plain yogurt to the same quantity of buttermilk. The results will be equally delicious.

Syrups and honeys – pure maple syrup, golden/light corn syrup, treacle and honey are all gluten-free and are delicious sweeteners in baking recipes.

Oats – not all people who are intolerant to gluten are able to eat oats. If in doubt, do not use them. However, there are many people who are intolerant to gluten who are able to eat oats, but make sure you choose brands labeled gluten-free to be safe.

Eggs – eggs do not contain gluten and are used in most of the recipes in this book. By separating the eggs and whisking the egg whites separately and folding into a cake batter, you can add additional air to your cakes, making them light and delicious.

Butter and fats – some margarines may contain gluten so it is best to use good quality unsalted butter in all recipes to remain gluten-free.

Alcohols – this can be a slightly confusing area for those who are gluten-intolerant. Beer is made with hops and so must be avoided. Some brands of whiskey (and cream-based whiskey liqueurs) may contain gluten from the caramel coloring which is added, although pure whiskey does not contain gluten. Before using any alcohol check with the manufacturer to ascertain whether it is gluten-free.

You've probably been there... A photo of a beautiful recipe entices you to start baking, only to discover your creation looks nothing like the photo. What went wrong? In this section, you'll find some basic strategies to help ensure that all of your gluten-free creations are as beautiful and delicious as the pictures that inspired you to make them—in this book and wherever else your gluten-free baking adventures lead you.

✓ Be a Follower First, an Adventurer Second

It's important to note that the recipes in this book have been thoroughly tested to ensure a consistent outcome. So the first rule of thumb when it comes to maximizing your success is to follow the recipes exactly as written. This means curbing any impulse to make substitutions or measurement changes, or to skip steps, as each of these changes will invariably impact the outcome of a recipe, often producing a less than desirable result. Instead, first make the recipe exactly as written. Then if you're feeling adventurous, make minor adjustments the next time around based on your taste preferences.

This is particularly important when it comes to baking. That's because the type of ingredients and how they are combined must be carefully planned to ensure they work together harmoniously to create the proper moisture, rise, and texture that make baked goods light, fluffy, and delicious.

✓ Use the Right Tools for the Job

Similarly, it's important to use the correct tools called for in a recipe. For example, if a recipe calls for an 8"×8" baking dish, substituting with a larger pan will result in a thinner baked good that may be overdone if the bake time is not adjusted. Also, using a whisk to do the job of a stand mixer (or electric hand mixer) will not only result in quite an upper-body workout, but may lead to ingredients not being properly combined, which will ultimately impact the outcome of a recipe.

✓ Remember Your Mise en Place

Mise en place is a French culinary term that refers to the practice of having each ingredient ready to go before you start making a recipe. That way, you don't have to stop to do anything other than add the next ingredient.

To get started, first read a recipe through in its entirety. This will help you determine what steps you need to do first in order to have all of the ingredients ready to go before you start combining them. For example, you may need to dice fruit for muffins, or cut butter into small pieces for scones. If you adopt the practice of gathering and preparing all of your ingredients in advance of starting a recipe, you will find life in the kitchen not only quicker and easier, but more successful and enjoyable too!

✓ Freshness Is Key!

For best results, fresh flour is essential. Gluten-free flour should ideally be purchased in sealed packages from a quality provider, since lengthy exposure to air can greatly impact freshness and moisture levels. Once you open a package of gluten-free flour, consider storing a 2-week supply in an airtight container in your pantry for convenience. Then store the remaining flour in an airtight container in the fridge or freezer to maintain long-term freshness. In general, gluten-free flours can be stored in the refrigerator for up to 1 month, and in the freezer for up to 6 months.

Note: If you store your flour in the refrigerator or freezer, be sure to bring it to room temperature before measuring it out in a recipe, since cold flour can negatively impact the outcome of a recipe.

✓ Know Your Oven

When it comes to baking, getting the best—and tastiest—results requires knowing your oven and how to properly use it.

One of the first things to determine is how accurate your oven is in reaching the proper temperature, since an oven that doesn't run true to temperature is often the cause of burnt biscuits or undercooked cakes. Using a quality oven thermometer can help you determine whether your oven runs hot, cold, or true to temperature.

Similarly, preheating your oven is a crucial step in baking success. It's highly important for an oven to be at proper baking temperature before a dish goes in for it to cook evenly. Additionally, try to resist the urge to continually open the oven door to check a dish's progress, since this allows a lot of heat to escape. If you know that your oven is true to temperature, it's best to wait until the minimum bake time is reached before opening the oven door to check. The exception, of course, is when a peek through the window reveals a dish that's browning sooner than expected.

And last, but not least. For the recipes in this book, unless otherwise specified, your oven rack should be placed in the middle position for even baking. This is especially important when it comes to gluten-free ingredients like nut flours and honey, which can burn easily.

Ready Set Bake

CHAPTER 2. Recipes
MUFFINS
Banana-Nut Muffins

Prep time: 15 minutes

Cooking time: 20 minutes

Servings: 12

Nutrients per serving:

Carbohydrates – 34.4 g

Fat – 9.8 g

Protein – 7.3 g

Calories – 254

Ingredients:

- ½ cup brown sugar or honey
- ½ cup olive oil
- 2-4 well-ripened bananas, mashed
- 2 eggs
- 2 Tbsp lemon or orange juice
- ½ cup GF hazelnut milk
- 1 cup rice flour baking mix
- 1 cup quinoa flour
- ½ tsp salt
- 1 tsp baking powder
- ½ cup soya granules
- ½ cup chopped plain walnuts or GF currants
- Ground dried orange peel

Instructions:

1. Preheat oven to 350°F.
2. Grease muffin tin cups or paper muffin cup liners, or a 7-inch square baking pan.
3. Cream sugar and olive oil.
4. Beat the mashed bananas with the eggs until they are fluffy. Add to creamed sugar mixture.
5. Stir in lemon or orange juice and hazelnut milk.
6. Add dry ingredients.
7. Mix just until blended. Do not overbeat; these are delicate.
8. Spoon into prepared muffin tins or into baking pan.
9. Bake at 350°F, about 20 minutes, or until light brown.
10. Sprinkle ground dried orange peel on top.

Quinoa Morning Muffins

Prep time: 15 minutes

Cooking time: 25 minutes

Servings: 20

Nutrients per serving:

Carbohydrates – 20.7 g

Fat – 16 g

Protein – 4.5 g

Calories – 246

Ingredients:

- 1 cup quinoa flour (or select two types using ½ cup of each: quinoa, millet, or amaranth)
- 1 cup rice flour
- 2 tsp xanthan gum
- 3 tsp baking powder
- 1 tsp baking soda
- ½ tsp cream of tartar
- ½ tsp salt
- ½ cup sugar
- 2 tsp cinnamon
- 1 tsp nutmeg
- 3 eggs beaten
- ½ cup milk, hot
- 1 cup olive oil or 1 cup butter, melted
- ½ cup plain walnuts, chopped, optional

Instructions:

1. Preheat oven to 400°F.
2. Grease bottoms of muffin tin cups with olive oil spray or paper muffin cup liners.
3. Mix dry ingredients together.
4. Add nuts, if you chose to.
5. Make a well in the dry ingredients and stir in liquids.
6. Spoon batter into muffin tin, half full.
7. Bake at 400°F for 25 minutes.

Buckwheat-Corn Muffins

Prep time: 15 minutes

Cooking time: 20 minutes

Servings: 12

Nutrients per serving:

Carbohydrates – 34.4 g

Fat – 5.9 g

Protein – 7.3 g

Calories – 136

Ingredients:

- 2 eggs, beaten
- 1½ cups milk
- 4 Tbsp butter, melted
- 1 cup buckwheat flour
- ½ cup yellow or white cornmeal
- 2 tsp baking powder
- ½ tsp salt
- ½ cup sugar

Instructions:

1. Preheat oven to 375°F.
2. Prepare muffin tins, lining with paper cups (oiled) or oiling nonstick muffin tin.
3. Combine dry ingredients.
4. Combine wet ingredients, then add to wet ingredients, stirring gently.
5. Spoon batter into muffin tins.
6. Bake at 375°F for 15-20 minutes or until toothpick comes out clean.
7. Remove muffins from tin; cool on rack.

Quinoa Flakes Muffins

Prep time: 15 minutes

Cooking time: 25 minutes

Servings: 20

Nutrients per serving:

Carbohydrates – 10.2 g

Fat – 4.7 g

Protein – 2.3 g

Calories – 93

Ingredients:

- ½ cup quinoa flakes
- ½ cup quinoa flour
- ½ cup flaxseed meal
- 2 tsp baking powder
- 1 tsp baking soda
- ½ tsp salt
- ½ cup orange juice
- 4 Tbsp butter, melted
- 2 ripe bananas
- 4 egg yolks

Instructions:

1. Preheat oven to 400°F.
2. Grease bottoms of muffin-tin cups or paper muffin cup liners.
3. Mix dry ingredients together.
4. Mix wet ingredients together.
5. Make a well in dry ingredients and stir in wet ingredients.
6. Spoon batter into muffin tin, half full.
7. Bake at 400°F for 25 minutes.

Sorghum Scones

Prep time: 15 minutes

Cooking time: 15 minutes

Servings: 12

Nutrients per serving:

Carbohydrates – 30.7 g

Fat – 2.9 g

Protein – 4 g

Calories – 192

Ingredients:

- 1½ cups sorghum flour
- ½ cup tapioca flour
- ½ cup rice flour
- 1½ tsp cream of tartar
- ½ tsp baking soda
- 1 tsp xanthan or guar gum
- 3 heaping Tbsp cumin
- ½ tsp salt
- 2 Tbsp sugar
- ½ cup currants or raisins
- 4 Tbsp butter
- 2 eggs, lightly beaten
- ½ cup plain GF yogurt or ½ cup milk (to brush on scones before baking)

Instructions:

1. Preheat oven to 450°F.
2. Grease baking sheet with oil or cover sheet with oiled tin foil.
3. Mix all dry ingredients.
4. Add butter to sugar and cream by pressing mix against the side of the mixing bowl.
5. Add beaten eggs and yogurt to butter and sugar.
6. Add the flour mixture to the egg mixture and stir lightly, just until all dry and wet ingredients are mixed together.
7. Add either currants or raisins and stir to blend in.
8. Either spoon out into big mounds on baking sheet or pat and roll the dough into a log. Brush with milk, this will enhance browning.
9. Bake for 12—15 minutes. Cut circle into wedges.

Teff Muffins

Prep time: 15 minutes

Cooking time: 25 minutes

Servings: 8

Nutrients per serving:

Carbohydrates – 32.4 g

Fat – 10.9 g

Protein – 4 g

Calories – 245

Ingredients:

- ½ cup teff flour
- ½ cup rice flour
- ½ cup tapioca flour
- 2 tsp baking powder
- ½ tsp cream of tartar
- 2 tsp cinnamon
- ½ tsp sea salt
- 2 eggs, slightly beaten
- ½ cup olive oil
- ½ cup GF soy milk
- ½ cup dried currants

Instructions:

1. Preheat oven to 400°F.
2. Grease muffin-tin paper liners.
3. Mix dry ingredients together.
4. Blend wet ingredients together in separate bowl.
5. Add wet ingredients to dry.
6. Fill muffin cups three-quarters full, bake for 25 minutes.

Honey Muffins

Prep time: 15 minutes

Cooking time: 25 minutes

Servings: 12

Nutrients per serving:

Carbohydrates – 14.9 g

Fat – 11 g

Protein – 2.3 g

Calories – 168

Ingredients:

- 1½ cups hazelnut flour
- ½ cup brown rice flour
- 2 tsp baking powder
- ½ cup honey
- 2/3 cup hazelnut milk
- 1 container (3.5 oz) prunebaby food
- 3½ Tbsp butter, melted.

Instructions:

1. Preheat oven to 375°F.
2. Grease muffin pan.
3. Mix together hazelnut flour, rice flour, and baking powder.
4. Add honey, hazelnut milk, prunes, and butter. Stir until well blended.
5. Fill muffin tins two-thirds full.
6. Bake at 375°F for 25 minutes.

Cornbread Muffins

Prep time: 15 minutes

Cooking time: 15 minutes

Servings: 12

Nutrients per serving:

Carbohydrates – 24.9 g

Fat – 8.5 g

Protein – 24.9 g

Calories – 191

Ingredients:

- 1 cup buttermilk
- 2 eggs, beaten
- ½ cup butter, melted
- ½ cup maple syrup
- 1½ cups yellow cornmeal
- ½ cup cornstarch
- 2 tsp baking powder
- ½ tsp baking soda
- ½ tsp salt
- ½ tsp cream of tartar
- ½ cup plain nuts, chopped

Instructions:

1. Preheat oven to 425°F.
2. Grease bottoms only of muffin tin cups or paper muffin cups.
3. Combine wet ingredients.
4. Combine dry ingredients.
5. Mix wet and dry ingredients together.
6. Bake at 425°F for 15 minutes.

Hot Herb and Spice Muffins

Prep time: 15 minutes

Cooking time: 15 minutes

Servings: 20

Nutrients per serving:

Carbohydrates – 9 g

Fat – 4.6 g

Protein – 3.9 g

Calories – 94

Ingredients:

- 3 eggs, separated
- 1½ cups buttermilk
- 2 Tbsp olive oil
- 1 cup brown rice flour
- 1 cup teff flour
- 1 tsp baking powder
- ½ tsp baking soda
- ½ tsp mustard powder
- ½ tsp garlic powder
- 1 tsp finely chopped fresh basil or marjoram
- ½ tsp oregano, dried or fresh
- ½ tsp dill seeds, smashed
- 1 Tbsp finely chopped onion
- ½ tsp cayenne pepper
- ½ tsp salt, optional
- 2 tsp finely chopped fresh parsley
- 1 cup grated Cheddar cheese

Instructions:

1. Preheat oven to 350°F.
2. Spray muffin-tin liners with oil.
3. Mix egg yolks with fork.
4. Beat egg whites until loosely stiff.
5. Mix all ingredients except eggs and cheese in saucepan and simmer for 3 minutes, stirring. Remove from heat and let cool. Add 2 Tbsp of this batter to the egg yolks, and stir in the cheese.
6. Add yolk-and-cheese mixture to other ingredients.
7. Gently fold egg whites into mixture.
8. Spoon into well-oiled muffin tin liners, filling three-quarters full.
9. Bake at 350°F for 15 minutes.

Gingerbread Muffins

Prep time: 15 minutes

Cooking time: 15 minutes

Servings: 12

Nutrients per serving:

Carbohydrates – 15.5 g

Fat – 1.1 g

Protein – 2.8 g

Calories – 84

Ingredients:

- ½ cup teff flour or buckwheat flour
- ½ tsp baking powder
- ½ tsp salt
- 3 tsp cinnamon
- 3 tsp ground ginger
- ½ tsp ground cloves
- 2 Tbsp brown sugar
- 2 Tbsp granulated sugar
- 2 egg yolks
- 3 Tbsp dark unsulfured molasses
- ½ cup orange juice
- 1 tsp orange peel
- 2 Tbsp freshly grated ginger
- 4 egg whites

Instructions:

1. Preheat oven to 400°F.
2. Grease bottoms of muffin tins or paper muffin cup liners.
3. Whisk together dry ingredients, except sugars.
4. Cream together egg yolks and brown sugar until it looks like a yellow ribbon.
5. Add molasses, orange juice, orange peel, and ginger.
6. Add wet ingredients, except egg whites, to dry ingredients.
7. Beat egg whites until soft peaks form.
8. Beat granulated sugar into the egg whites, 1 Tbsp at a time.
9. Fold egg-white mixture into batter.
10. Fill muffin tins three-quarters full.
11. Bake at 400°F for 15-18 minutes.

PANCAKES

Cinnamon Apple Crêpes

Prep time: 15 minutes

Cooking time: 15 minutes

Servings: 12

Nutrients per serving:

Carbohydrates – 15.5 g

Fat – 1.1 g

Protein – 2.8 g

Calories – 84

Ingredients:

- 4 egg yolks, beaten
- 2 whole eggs, beaten
- 1 cup milk
- 2 Tbsp butter, melted
- ½ cup tapioca flour
- ½ cup cornstarch
- ½ cup sorghum flour
- 2 Tbsp sugar
- ½ tsp salt
- ½ tsp xanthan gum

Apple Crêpe Topping:

- 2 Tbsp cornstarch
- ½ cup water
- ½ cup sugar
- ½ tsp cinnamon
- 5 cooking apples, peeled, cored, and thinly sliced
- ½ cup plain walnuts, chopped

Instructions:

1. Mix beaten egg yolks and whole eggs.
2. Blend milk and butter in a separate bowl.
3. Combine flours, sugar, salt, and gum.
4. Alternately add egg and butter mixtures to flour mixture, making a thin batter.
5. Refrigerate for an hour or overnight before cooking on your griddle.
6. To make the apple topping, put all ingredients in a skillet, stir and let simmer for a 10 minutes over medium heat.

Herb Crêpes

Prep time: 15 minutes

Cooking time: 10 minutes

Servings: 12

Nutrients per serving:

Carbohydrates – 14.7 g

Fat – 7.9 g

Protein – 6.5 g

Calories – 157

Ingredients:

- 1 cup amaranth flour
- 1 cup soy flour
- 1 tsp fresh or dried tarragon
- 1 tsp chopped parsley
- 1 tsp chives
- 3 eggs
- 1 cup beer
- 1 cup GF chicken bouillon
- ½ cup butter, melted
- 1 Tbsp GF sour cream

Instructions:

1. Blend dry ingredients.
2. Beat eggs.
3. Combine all wet ingredients.
4. Add wet ingredients to dry.
5. Spoon or ladle onto a hot griddle.
6. Cook until brown, 5 minutes each side.

Chocolate Dessert Crêpe

Prep time: 15 minutes

Cooking time: 10 minutes

Servings: 8

Nutrients per serving:

Carbohydrates – 24.9 g

Fat – 9.7 g

Protein – 6.6 g

Calories – 213

Ingredients:

- 3 Tbsp butter
- 1½ cups buttermilk
- 3 eggs, beaten
- 2 ounces GF bittersweet chocolate
- 1 Tbsp ground cardamom
- 1 cup sorghum flour
- ½ Tbsp baking soda
- 3 Tbsp sugar
- 3 Tbsp good quality pure cocoa
- ½ tsp salt

Instructions:

1. Melt butter and chocolate with cardamom in a double boiler.
2. Combine buttermilk and eggs in a separate bowl.
3. Combine dry ingredients.
4. Pour alternately the buttermilk mixture and the melted chocolate mixture into the dry ingredients.
5. Let batter sit for ½ hour.
6. Cook on a greased hot griddle.

Apple Pancakes

Prep time: 15 minutes

Cooking time: 5 minutes

Servings: 10

Nutrients per serving:

Carbohydrates – 18.5 g

Fat – 1.9 g

Protein – 3.2 g

Calories – 104

Ingredients:

- 1 cup milk
- 2 eggs, whisked
- 1 apple
- 1 cup rice flour
- ½ cup sorghum flour
- 1 tsp baking powder
- 1 tsp cinnamon, plus 1 tsp for topping
- 1 tsp sugar, plus 1 tsp for topping

Instructions:

1. Peel and core apple, then slice it in thin horizontal slices.
2. Mix milk and eggs together.
3. Blend flours, baking powder, cinnamon, and sugar.
4. Add flour mixture to milk mixture, a little at a time, until batter thickens.
5. Pour mixture into oiled, hot frying pan. Lay a few apple slices on top. Cook for about five minutes
6. To serve, mix 1 tsp each cinnamon and sugar together for topping. Sprinkle over the cooked pancake.

Buckwheat Pancakes

Prep time: 15 minutes

Cooking time: 5 minutes

Servings: 10

Nutrients per serving:

Carbohydrates – 18.3 g

Fat – 2.9 g

Protein – 2.3 g

Calories – 109

Ingredients:

- 1 cup buckwheat flour
- ½ cup rice flour
- ½ tsp sea salt
- 1 tsp baking powder
- ½ tsp xanthan gum
- 2 Tbsp unsulfured molasses
- 1 egg, beaten
- 1½ cups GF rice milk
- 2 Tbsp butter, melted
- 1 tsp vinegar

Instructions:

1. Mix dry ingredients together.
2. Mix wet ingredients in separate bowl.
3. Lightly stir dry ingredients into wet. Let sit for 5 minutes.
4. Ladle batter onto your hot griddle.Cook for 2-3 minutes. Flip and cook for another 2-3 minutes.

Quinoa Pancakes

Prep time: 15 minutes

Cooking time: 15 minutes

Servings: 10

Nutrients per serving:

Carbohydrates – 20.4 g

Fat – 3.7 g

Protein – 2.4 g

Calories – 124

Ingredients:

- 1½ cups quinoa flour
- ½ cup rice flour
- 4 tsp baking powder
- ½ tsp cream of tartar
- ½ tsp salt
- 1 tsp xanthan gum
- 1 Tbsp honey
- 2 cups GF rice milk
- 2 Tbsp vegetable oil

Instructions:

1. Mix dry ingredients.
2. .Add liquids and lightly whisk to mix.
3. Batter may thicken as it stands. Add 1 or 2 Tbsp water, as needed, as you cook pancakes.
4. Ladle onto your hot griddle. Cook for 2-3 minutes. Flip and cook for another 2-3 minutes.

Tapioca Waffles with Cumin

Prep time: 15 minutes

Cooking time: 10 minutes

Servings: 8

Nutrients per serving:

Carbohydrates – 28 g

Fat – 8.4 g

Protein – 3.1 g

Calories – 199

Ingredients:

- 2 eggs, separated
- ½ cup oil
- 1 cup buttermilk
- ½ cup rice flour
- 1 cup tapioca flour
- 1 tsp baking soda
- 1½ tsp baking powder
- 2 tsp brown sugar
- ½ tsp cumin

Instructions:

1. Preheat waffle iron or flat pan for stovetop cooking.
2. Beat egg whites and set aside.
3. Mix together dry ingredients.
4. Slightly beat egg yolks together in a small bowl.
5. Blend oil and buttermilk into the egg yolks.
6. Mix egg yolk mixture into the dry ingredients.
7. Fold in egg whites. Bake in a waffle iron or cook as pancakes for about 10 minutes.

Soy Griddle Cakes

Prep time: 15 minutes

Cooking time: 5 minutes

Servings: 6

Nutrients per serving:

Carbohydrates – 22.4 g

Fat – 8 g

Protein – 19.1 g

Calories – 237

Ingredients:

- ½ cup soy flour
- ½ cup soya granules
- ½ tsp baking soda
- 3 Tbsp honey
- 2 eggs
- 1 cup GF soy milk

Instructions:

1. Oil skillet lightly.
2. Mix all ingredients. Allow to stand for 5 minutes.
3. Form patties.
4. Brown on each side in skillet for about 5 minutes.
5. Serve with jam.

Potato Pancakes

Prep time: 15 minutes

Cooking time: 10 minutes

Servings: 12

Nutrients per serving:

Carbohydrates – 13.2 g

Fat – 3.5 g

Protein – 3 g

Calories – 96

Ingredients:

- 3 potatoes, raw, grated
- 1 medium zucchini, grated
- ½ cup carrots, grated
- ½ cup onion, finely chopped
- ½ cup garbanzo flour
- ½ cup potato flour
- ½ tsp salt
- 1 tsp baking powder
- 1 tsp dill weed
- 1 Tbsp yellow curry
- 2 eggs, beaten
- 2 Tbsp olive or canola oil
- ½ cup white wine

Instructions:

1. Combine potatoes, zucchini, carrots, and onion.
2. Add beaten eggs and oil; stir to combine.
3. Mix the dry ingredients in a separate bowl, then add to potato mixture.
4. Add the wine to desired consistency—may need less.
5. Spoon or ladle onto a hot griddle; brown on both sides for 7-10 minutes.

Coconut Pancakes

Prep time: 15 minutes

Cooking time: 10 minutes

Servings: 4

Nutrients per serving:

Carbohydrates – 51.8 g

Fat – 16.7 g

Protein – 10.1 g

Calories – 398

Ingredients:

- ½ cup unsweetened coconut flakes
- ½ cup sorghum flour
- 1 cup GF oat flour
- 2 tsp GF baking powder
- ½ tsp cream of tartar
- ½ tsp salt
- 2 cups GF rice milk
- 2 Tbsp butter, melted
- 2 eggs
- 2 Tbsp honey

Instructions:

1. Mix dry ingredients in bowl.
2. Add liquids and whisk to mix.
3. Let stand for 15 minutes.
4. Preheat griddle, grease as needed. Spoon batter onto hot griddle. Turn when edges seem dry. If batter thickens, add 1-2 Tbsp water to the batter as needed.

BREADS

Monkey Bread

Prep time: 25 minutes

Cooking time: 40 minutes

Servings: 12

Nutrients per serving:

Carbohydrates – 49.6 g

Fat – 6.8 g

Protein – 4.8 g

Calories – 279

Ingredients:

- 3 large eggs, lightly beaten
- ½ cup oil
- ½ cup plus 1 Tbsp water
- 1 cup buttermilk or sour milk
- 2 cups brown rice flour
- ½ cup potato starch
- ½ cup tapioca flour
- 3½ tsp xanthan gum
- ½ cup sugar
- 1½ tsp salt
- 1 package dry yeast
- Sweet Dust Coating
- ½ cup rice flour
- ¼ cup sugar
- 3 Tbsp cinnamon
- ¼ tsp salt

Instructions:

1. Preheat oven to 400°F.
2. Grease a Bundt pan or an 8-inch cake pan, using a spray of oil or a paper napkin saturated with oil.

3. Combine wet ingredients in a large bowl or baking pan of a bread maker.
4. Blend dry ingredients together, including the yeast, in a separate bowl.
5. Add well-blended dry ingredients to combined wet ingredients.
6. Select Normal/White cycle for bread machine.
7. Mix all ingredients in the bread machine—use a rubber spatula to scrape the inside edges of the bread machine to incorporate all the mixture. Alternatively, mix all ingredients by hand; let rise till doubled in size.
8. Remove bread pan after first bake cycle.
9. Combine Sweet Dust Coating ingredients.
10. Roll fistfuls of risen dough lightly in sweet coating.
11. Put the rolls in the cake pan, stuffing all coated balls side by side. (You can knead the remains of the flour, sugar, and cinnamon with softened butter and then sprinkle over tops of the monkey rolls.)
12. Bake at 400°F for 40 minutes, until a knife comes out clean.

Yeast Bread with Molasses

Prep time: 25 minutes

Cooking time: 40 minutes

Servings: 16 slices

Nutrients per serving:

Carbohydrates – 32.1 g

Fat – 4.1 g

Protein – 3.9 g

Calories – 181

Ingredients:

- 1 cup brown rice flour
- 1 cup white rice flour
- ½ cup tapioca flour
- ½ cup potato starch flour
- ½ cup kasha, ground slightly in coffee grinder
- 2½ tsp xanthan gum
- 1½ tsp table salt
- 3 eggs, lightly beaten
- 1½ cups water
- 1 tsp vinegar or 1½ tsp dough enhancer (lemon)
- 3 Tbsp olive oil or butter
- 1 Tbsp molasses
- 3 Tbsp sugar
- 1 Tbsp dry yeast

Instructions:

1. Blend together the flours, kasha, xanthan gum, and salt.
2. Combine the eggs, water, vinegar or dough enhancer, oil, and molasses.
3. Stir together the sugar and yeast.
4. Place the ingredients in the baking pan.
5. Bake in oven at 350°F for 40 minutes until brown.

Brown and White Rice Bread

Prep time: 25 minutes

Cooking time: 1 hour

Servings: 15 slices

Nutrients per serving:

Carbohydrates – 36.5 g

Fat – 0 g

Protein – 5.1 g

Calories – 215

Ingredients:

- 2½ cups white rice flour
- 1 cup brown rice flour
- 2½ tsp xanthan gum
- 3 Tbsp sugar
- 1½ tsp salt
- ½ cup dry milk
- 2 packages active dry yeast
- ½ cup golden raisins
- 3 eggs, lightly beaten
- 1 tsp cider vinegar
- 3 Tbsp canola oil
- 1½ cups water

Instructions:

1. Preheat oven to 325°F. Grease bottom of 9 x 5 x 3-inch loaf pan.
2. Mix the dry and wet ingredients in separate bowls.
3. Add wet ingredients to dry and stir just until it reaches the consistency of cake batter.
4. Put in loaf pan.
5. Proof for 15 minutes in a warm oven. Let it rise.
6. Bake in oven at 325°F for 1 hour.

Chickpea Yeast Bread

Prep time: 15 minutes

Cooking time: 1 hour

Servings: 15 slices

Nutrients per serving:

Carbohydrates – 30.8 g

Fat – 5.6 g

Protein – 4.9 g

Calories – 194

Ingredients:

- 3 large eggs, lightly beaten
- 1 tsp cider vinegar
- 3 Tbsp olive oil
- 1½ cups water
- 1 tsp pure maple syrup
- 1 cup chickpea flour
- 1 cup brown rice flour
- 1 cup tapioca flour
- ½ cup cornstarch
- 3 tsp xanthan gum
- 3 Tbsp brown sugar
- 2 tsp sea salt
- ½ cup dry milk
- 1 package dry yeast

Instructions:

1. Grease bottom of 9 x 5 x 3-inch loaf pan.
2. Mix the dry and wet ingredients in separate bowls.
3. Add wet ingredients to dry and stir just until cake-batter consistency.
4. Put in loaf pan.
5. Proof for 45 minutes or longer in a barely warm oven; let rise slightly.
6. Remove from oven and let stand for 15 minutes.
7. Preheat oven to 325°F.
8. Bake for 1 hour. If it browns too quickly, cover with a piece of aluminum foil, shiny-side up.

Farmhouse Sour Milk Yeast Bread

Prep time: 25 minutes

Cooking time: 1 hour

Servings: 15 slices

Nutrients per serving:

Carbohydrates – 33.4 g

Fat – 7.7 g

Protein – 6.8 g

Calories – 231

Ingredients:

- 3 large eggs, lightly beaten
- ½ cup oil
- ½ cup plus 1 Tbsp water
- 1 cup buttermilk
- 1 cup garbanzo and/or fava bean flour
- 1 cup millet flour
- ½ cup potato starch
- ½ cup tapioca flour
- 3½ tsp xanthan gum
- ½ cup sugar
- 1½ tsp salt
- 2 tsp powdered eggs
- 1 package dry yeast

Instructions:

1. Grease 9 x 5 x 3-inch loaf pan.
2. Mix the wet ingredients together.
3. Mix the dry ingredients together in a separate bowl.
4. Add blended dry ingredient to blended wet ingredients, bit by bit, by hand. Stir just until combined.
5. Put in loaf pan.
6. Proof at room temperature all day or in a warm oven for 45 minutes until it rises.
7. Preheat oven to 325°F.
8. Bake at for 1 hour.

Cranberry Yeast Bread

Prep time: 15 minutes

Cooking time: 10 minutes

Servings: 16 slices

Nutrients per serving:

Carbohydrates – 30.1 g

Fat – 5.9 g

Protein – 5.8 g

Calories – 197

Ingredients:

- 3 Tbsp sugar
- 1 cup white rice flour
- 2 cups millet, sorghum, or amaranth flour
- ¼ cup soy flour
- 1 Tbsp xanthan gum
- 1½ tsp salt
- ½ cup dry milk
- 1 package dry yeast
- 1 cup dried or fresh cranberries or currants
- 3 large eggs, lightly beaten
- 1 tsp cider vinegar
- 3 Tbsp oil
- 1½ cups water
- 4 Tbsp honey

Instructions:

1. Preheat oven to 350°F.
2. Grease 9 x 5 x 3- inch loaf pan.
3. Mix dry ingredients together.
4. Mix wet ingredients together.
5. Add dry ingredients to the wet ingredients bit by bit. Stir by hand.
6. Place in prepared loaf pan.
7. Let rise all day or overnight.
8. Cut diagonal slashes into the top of the loaf.
9. Bake at 350°F for 45 minutes. Turn on side to rest after baking.

Pumpkin Yeast Bread

Prep time: 25 minutes

Cooking time: 45 minutes

Servings: 16 slices

Nutrients per serving:

Carbohydrates – 31.7 g

Fat – 9.2 g

Protein – 4.9 g

Calories – 228

Ingredients:

- ½ cup warm water
- 2 cups fresh pumpkin, cooked and mashed
- 2 cups apple juice, heated to hot in microwave
- ½ cup canola oil
- ½ tsp sugar
- 2 packages dry powdered yeast
- 2 cups quinoa flour
- 1 cup soy flour
- ½ cup tapioca flour
- ½ cup garbanzo and/or fava bean flour
- 3 tsp xanthan gum
- 2 Tbsp brown sugar
- 1 tsp cumin
- 2 tsp salt
- ½ cup golden raisins

Instructions:

1. Preheat oven to 350°F.
2. Grease 9 x 5 x 3- inch loaf pan.
3. Add warm water and sugar to yeast in a glass measuring cup, cover, and let it proof.
4. Combine dry ingredients.
5. Combine pumpkin, apple juice, oil, and raisins.
6. Stir dry ingredients into pumpkin mixture until the dough looks like cake batter.
7. Place dough in prepared loaf pan.
8. Proof with a cloth over dough at room temperature until dough comes to the top of the pan.
9. Bake 45 minutes.

Indian Ricegrass Yeast Bread

Prep time: 25 minutes

Cooking time: 50 minutes

Servings: 15 slices

Nutrients per serving:

Carbohydrates – 23.2 g

Fat – 8.6 g

Protein – 5 g

Calories – 191

Ingredients:

- 2 tsp dry yeast
- 1 cup GF Montina (Indian ricegrass) flour
- 1 cup brown rice flour
- ½ cup soy flour
- ½ cup cornmeal or quinoa flour
- 1½ tsp sea salt
- ½ cup sunflower seeds, ground
- 2½ cups water
- ½ cup canola oil
- 1½ Tbsp honey
- Topping:
- 2 Tbsp butter, melted
- 2 Tbsp pure sesame seeds

Instructions:

1. Dissolve yeast in warm water. Let rise.
2. Stir oil and honey into risen yeast mixture.
3. Mix flours, salt, and ground sunflower seeds together.
4. Add three-quarters of the flour mixture to the oil-honey-yeast mixture; then add more gradually until dough is smooth and elastic.
5. Let rise in bowl for 1 hour until doubled in height. Punch down. Add a bit more white rice flour, knead and form into loaves.
6. Let rise again in a warm place, 45 minutes, with a damp cloth over it.
7. Preheat oven to 400°F.
8. Top loaves with melted butter and sesame seeds. Bake for 50 minutes.

Buckwheat Yeast Bread

Prep time: 20 minutes

Cooking time: 45 minutes

Servings: 12 slices

Nutrients per serving:

Carbohydrates – 20.8 g

Fat – 5.3 g

Protein – 3.5 g

Calories – 145

Ingredients:

- ½ cup (60 ml) water, very warm
- 3 eggs, beaten
- 1½ cups milk
- 2 Tbsp unsulfured molasses
- 3 Tbsp butter, melted
- ½ cup buckwheat flour
- ½ cup tapioca flour
- 1 package (0.25oz) dry yeast
- Pinch sugar
- 1½ cups brown rice flour
- ½ cup potato starch
- 1 tsp sea salt
- 1 Tbsp xanthan gum
- 1 tsp cardamom

Instructions:

1. Grease 9 x 5 x 3-inch loaf pan.
2. Mix yeast, sugar, and water in a glass measuring cup. Cover with a paper towel and let the yeast rise to the top of the cup.
3. Stir yeast mixture into beaten eggs.
4. Add milk, molasses, and melted butter.
5. Add dry ingredients into wet, a third at a time, stirring with a large wooden spoon or your hands until the batter becomes rich and cake-like.
6. Cover with a damp cloth and let rise all day or overnight at room temperature. It will taste better the longer it proofs.
7. Preheat oven to 400°F.
8. Score top of the risen loaf with diagonal cuts.
9. Bake the loaf for about 30-45 minutes.

Mock Black Russian Yeast Bread

Prep time: 20 minutes

Cooking time: 4 hours

Servings: 16 slices

Nutrients per serving:

Carbohydrates – 31.3 g

Fat – 5.8 g

Protein – 4.5 g

Calories – 196

Ingredients:

- 3 eggs
- 1 tsp cider vinegar
- 3 Tbsp olive oil
- 2 Tbsp molasses
- 1½ cups water
- 2 cups brown rice flour
- ½ cup potato starch
- ½ cup tapioca flour
- ½ cup rice bran
- 1 Tbsp xanthan gum
- 3 tsp dark brown sugar
- 1½ tsp salt
- ½ cup dry milk
- 1 Tbsp instant coffee
- 4 ½ tsp pure cocoa
- 2 Tbsp caraway seeds
- 1 package dry yeast

Instructions:

1. Grease 9 x 5 x 3-inch loaf pan.
2. Mix wet ingredients together.
3. Whisk dry ingredients together.
4. Add the mixed dry ingredients to the mixed wet ingredients gradually, by hand. Stir well.
5. Put into prepared loaf pan.
6. Proof all day or overnight at room temperature.
7. Bake at 325°F for 3-4 hours. Test with a toothpick in the center.

Millet Bread

Prep time: 15 minutes

Cooking time: 30 minutes

Servings: 12 slices

Nutrients per serving:

Carbohydrates – 31.2 g

Fat – 6.1 g

Protein – 8 g

Calories – 212

Ingredients:

- 1 cup plain GF yogurt or buttermilk
- ½ cup butter
- ½ cup warm water
- 1 Tbsp honey
- 2 eggs, beaten
- 1 package dry yeast
- 2 cups millet flour
- ½ cup soy flour
- 2½ tsp xanthan gum
- ½ tsp salt
- ¾ cup millet seeds, crushed or ground, divided

Instructions:

1. Grease 9 x 5 x 3-inch loaf pan with canola oil.
2. Combine yogurt and butter in a saucepan over low heat, stirring, just until butter is melted.
3. Dissolve the yeast into the warm water.
4. Stir in honey and beaten eggs.
5. Mix yogurt and butter into the yeast mixture.
6. Add flours, xanthan gum, salt, and ½ cup millet seeds into the wet ingredients slowly, bit by bit, by hand.
7. Spoon dough into an oiled 9 x 5 x 3-inch bread pan.
8. Cover and let rise all day at room temperature.
9. Cut 2 diagonal slashes into top of loaf; sprinkle with remaining ¼ cup millet seeds.
10. Bake in preheated 375° F oven for 30 minutes

COOKIES

Nitty Gritty Cookies

Prep time: 15 minutes

Cooking time: 25 minutes

Servings: 20

Nutrients per serving:

Carbohydrates – 31.7 g

Fat – 15.6 g

Protein – 6.3 g

Calories – 293

Ingredients:

- ½ cup butter, softened
- ½ cup honey
- ½ cup apple juice
- 2 cups GF bread crumbs
- 1½ tsp salt
- 1 cup sesame seeds
- 1 cup sunflower seeds, roasted
- 1 cup quinoa flakes
- 1 cup plain walnuts, finely chopped
- 1 cup hazelnut flour
- 1 cup cornmeal
- 1 cup yellow raisins

Instructions:

1. Preheat oven to 350°F.
2. Prepare cookie sheet with either oil or parchment paper.
3. Cream butter and honey together, then mix in other ingredients except for the juice.
4. Add juice a little at a time until mixture holds together. If mixture is too sticky, add a little rice flour.
5. Shape into balls and place on an oiled or parchment-covered cookie sheet.
6. Bake for 25 minutes.

Hazelnut Cookies

Prep time: 15 minutes

Cooking time: 35 minutes

Servings: 20

Nutrients per serving:

Carbohydrates – 10.3 g

Fat – 7.2 g

Protein – 1.7 g

Calories – 113

Ingredients:

- ½ cup butter, softened
- 6 Tbsp maple syrup
- 2 tsp hazelnut flavoring or extract
- 3 Tbsp brown sugar
- 1 cup hazelnut flour
- ½ cup bean flour
- 1 cup quinoa flour
- ½ cup currants
- Cinnamon and sugar for dusting cookies after baking

Instructions:

1. Preheat oven to 325°F.
2. Grease cookie sheet.
3. Blend the butter, maple syrup, hazelnut flavoring, and brown sugar with a hand mixer until creamy.
4. Add the hazelnut flour, bean flour, and quinoa flour. Mix until the dough sticks together.
5. Add currants.
6. Form the dough into 1½-inch balls.
7. Place them on the prepared cookie sheet and bake for 30-35 minutes.
8. Remove from oven and let them cool or roll them in cinnamon sugar while still warm.

Almond Crispies

Prep time: 20 minutes

Cooking time: 10 minutes

Servings: 20

Nutrients per serving:

Carbohydrates – 9.8 g

Fat – 5.6 g

Protein – 1.6 g

Calories – 90

Ingredients:

- ½ cup rice flour
- ½ cup tapioca flour
- ½ cup almond meal
- ½ cup superfine sugar
- 1 tsp baking powder
- 1 tsp cinnamon
- ½ tsp sea salt
- ½ cup plain almonds, chopped
- ½ cup sweetened coconut
- ½ cup orange juice
- 4 Tbsp butter, softened
- 1 Tbsp warm water

Instructions:

1. Preheat oven to 375°F.
2. Lightly spray or grease cookie sheet.
3. Combine the dry ingredients in a bowl.
4. Combine the wet ingredients in another bowl.
5. Blend the wet and dry ingredients together, folding in the chopped almonds.
6. Drop spoonfuls of dough onto greased cookie sheet.
7. Bake 8-10 minutes, until lightly golden.
8. Let cookies set on baking sheet 10 minutes, then remove to cooling rack.

Old-Fashioned Almond Macaroons

Prep time: 20 minutes

Cooking time: 10 minutes

Servings: 20

Nutrients per serving:

Carbohydrates – 11.2 g

Fat – 5 g

Protein – 2.6 g

Calories – 100

Ingredients:

- 4 egg whites, unbeaten
- 1 tsp almond flavoring or extract
- ½ pound GF confectioners'sugar
- ½ pound plain almonds, ground (use coffee grinder)
- 1 tsp lemon zest

Instructions:

1. Preheat oven to 375°F.
2. Lightly spray or grease cookie sheet; set aside.
3. Combine the dry ingredients in a bowl.
4. Combine the wet ingredients in another bowl.
5. Blend the wet and dry ingredients together, folding in the chopped almonds.
6. Drop spoonfuls of dough onto greased cookie sheet.
7. Bake 8-10 minutes until lightly golden.
8. Let cookies set on baking sheet 10 minutes, then remove to cooling rack.

Almond Sugar Cookies

Prep time: 15 minutes

Cooking time: 30 minutes

Servings: 20

Nutrients per serving:

Carbohydrates – 11.4 g

Fat – 4.5 g

Protein – 2.5 g

Calories – 96

Ingredients:

- 2 egg whites
- 2 Tbsp lemon juice
- ½ tsp lemon extract
- ½ tsp almond extract
- ½ cup granulated sugar
- ½ tsp lemon zest
- 1 tsp cinnamon
- 1½ cups almond meal
- Plain whole almonds

Instructions:

1. Preheat oven to 250°F.
2. Beat egg whites until stiff, adding sugar gradually.
3. Blend lemon juice, lemon zest, lemon extract, almond extract, and cinnamon into egg white mixture.
4. Sprinkle almond meal on egg white mixture and fold in gently to blend.
5. Place on greased cookie sheet 1 inch apart.
6. Place 1 whole almond on top of each cookie.
7. Bake for 30 minutes.

Molasses Snaps

Prep time: 15 minutes

Cooking time: 30 minutes

Servings: 20

Nutrients per serving:

Carbohydrates – 22.4 g

Fat – 5 g

Protein – 2.4 g

Calories – 144

Ingredients:

- 2 egg whites
- 2 Tbsp lemon juice
- ½ tsp lemon extract
- ½ tsp almond extract
- ½ cup granulated sugar
- ½ tsp lemon zest
- 1 tsp cinnamon
- 1½ cups almond meal
- Plain whole almonds

Instructions:

1. Preheat oven to 375°F.
2. Line cookie sheet with brown paper or parchment paper.
3. Beat together butter, sugar, molasses, and eggs.
4. Add vanilla, mix well.
5. Sift together flours, soda, baking powder, salt, and spices. Add to batter, then beat until well mixed.
6. Drop by small amounts onto paper.
7. Flatten dough using the back of a wet wooden spoon dipped into sugar.
8. Bake until brown for 30 minutes.

Brownies

Prep time: 15 minutes

Cooking time: 25 minutes

Servings: 12

Nutrients per serving:

Carbohydrates – 28.4 g

Fat – 13 g

Protein – 3.6 g

Calories – 245

Ingredients:

- ¼ cup pure cocoa powder
- 1 cup sugar
- ½ tsp salt
- ½ cup tapioca flour
- ½ cup potato starch
- 1 tsp xanthan gum
- 1 tsp baking soda
- ½ cup plain walnuts, chopped
- ½ cup butter
- ½ cup milk
- 4 eggs
- 1 tsp vanilla flavoring or extract

Instructions:

1. Preheat oven to 350° F.
2. Butter bottom of 9-inch square pan or line with waxed paper and grease, leaving sides ungreased, which allows batter to climb.
3. Mix butter and cocoa in a bowl over hot water (double-boiler style).

4. Blend dry ingredients, then add to chocolate mixture.
5. Blend wet ingredients, then add to chocolate batter.
6. Add chopped walnuts.
7. Pour into prepared pan.
8. Bake for 25 minutes.
9. Test with toothpick for desired doneness. Cool before cutting.

Carob Brownies

Prep time: 20 minutes

Cooking time: 25 minutes

Servings: 20

Nutrients per serving:

Carbohydrates – 23.5 g

Fat – 5.4 g

Protein – 2.2 g

Calories – 151

Ingredients:

- ½ cup butter
- 1 cup honey
- 2 eggs
- 3 tsp vanilla flavoring or extract
- 5 Tbsp roasted GF carob powder
- ½ cup rice flour
- 1½ tsp baking powder
- 1 tsp xanthan gum
- ½ tsp salt
- ½ cup plain walnuts, chopped

Instructions:

1. Preheat oven to 350° F.
2. Butter bottom of 9-inch square pan or line with waxed paper and grease, leaving sides ungreased, which allows batter to climb.
3. Mix butter and cocoa in a bowl over hot water (double-boiler style).
4. Blend dry ingredients, then add to chocolate mixture.
5. Blend wet ingredients, then add to chocolate batter.
6. Add chopped walnuts.
7. Pour into prepared pan.
8. Bake for 25 minutes.
9. Test with toothpick for desired doneness. Cool before cutting.

Chocolate Coconut Macaroons

Prep time: 15 minutes

Cooking time: 20 minutes

Servings: 20

Nutrients per serving:

Carbohydrates – 5.7 g

Fat – 3.1 g

Protein – 1 g

Calories – 54

Ingredients:

- ½ cup sweetened condensed milk
- 1 tsp vanilla flavoring or extract
- 1-ounce square GF baking chocolate
- 1½ cups shredded sweetened coconut

Instructions:

1. Preheat oven to 350°F.
2. Spray cookie sheets with nonstick cooking spray.
3. Melt chocolate in top of double boiler. Remove from the boiler.
4. Add condensed milk, coconut, and vanilla.
5. Drop on greased cookie sheet.
6. Bake for 15-20 minutes.

Quinoa Applesauce Cookies

Prep time: 20 minutes

Cooking time: 20 minutes

Servings: 20

Nutrients per serving:

Carbohydrates – 13.7 g

Fat – 6.3 g

Protein – 1.6 g

Calories – 118

Ingredients:

- ½ cup plain pecans, ground
- 1 cup currants or dried apples
- 1½ cups quinoa flour, divided
- ½ tsp baking soda
- ½ tsp baking powder
- ½ tsp salt
- ½ tsp ground cloves
- 1 tsp xanthan gum
- ½ cup unsalted butter
- ½ cup maple syrup
- 1 large egg, beaten
- 2 cups applesauce

Instructions:

1. Preheat oven to 350°F.
2. Line cookie sheets with parchment paper.
3. Combine ground nuts with dried fruit.
4. Sprinkle ¼ cup quinoa flour over fruit and nuts; toss until they are coated. Set aside.

5. Blend remaining dry ingredients.
6. Mix butter, maple syrup, beaten egg, and applesauce in a separate bowl.
7. Combine wet ingredients with dry. Stir well.
8. Fold in nut mixture lightly.
9. Spoon the batter onto cookie sheets.
10. Bake for 20 minutes.

Sesame Seed Butter Cookies

Prep time: 20 minutes

Cooking time: 10 minutes

Servings: 100

Nutrients per serving:

Carbohydrates – 5.9 g

Fat – 2.2 g

Protein – 1 g

Calories – 45

Ingredients:

- ½ cup butter
- 2 cups light brown sugar
- 1 egg, beaten
- ½ cup sorghum flour, sifted
- ½ cup potato starch
- 1 Tbsp tapioca flour
- ½ tsp baking powder
- 1 tsp xanthan gum
- ½ tsp salt
- 1 tsp vanilla flavoring or extract
- ½ cup sesame seeds, toasted
- ½ cup plain sesame seeds for topping

Instructions:

1. Preheat oven to 325°F.
2. Grease a cookie sheet; cover with parchment paper.
3. Cream butter and sugar well in a large bowl.
4. Add the beaten egg.
5. Sift together the presifted flours, baking powder, xanthan gum, and salt.
6. Add dry ingredients to butter-sugar-egg mixture.
7. Blend the vanilla and toasted sesame seeds into batter until well mixed.
8. Drop by tsp, or less, on parchment-covered cookie sheet.
9. Sprinkle tops of unbaked cookies with plain sesame seeds.
10. Bake for 8-10 minutes or until light brown. Wafers cook quickly, so check often.
11. Allow to cool 1 minute before removing from pan.

Chocolate Muddy Buddies

Prep time: 25 minutes

Cooking time: 10 minutes

Servings: 40

Nutrients per serving:

Carbohydrates – 8.4 g

Fat – 3.6 g

Protein – 1.2 g

Calories – 70

Ingredients:

- ½ cup peanut butter
- ½ cup butter
- 1 tsp vanilla flavoring or extract
- 1 cup GF semisweet chocolate chips
- 9 cups GF puffed rice cereal
- 1 cup GF confectioners' sugar

Instructions:

1. Melt chocolate chips, peanut butter, and butter on stove over low heat. Stir until smooth.
2. Add vanilla to chocolate mixture.
3. Pour melted chocolate mixture over cereal and stir to coat well.
4. Put the powdered sugar into a brown paper bag.
5. Pour chocolate-coated cereal into the bag containing the powdered sugar.
6. Shake the bag to coat the cereal.
7. Spread mixture out on waxed paper to cool.

French Lace Cookies

Prep time: 25 minutes

Cooking time: 6 minutes

Servings: 10

Nutrients per serving:

Carbohydrates – 30.8 g

Fat – 14.4 g

Protein – 1.1 g

Calories – 257

Ingredients:

- ½ cup unsalted butter
- ½ cup corn syrup
- ½ cup brown sugar
- ½ cup tapioca flour
- ½ cup arrowroot
- ½ tsp xanthan gum
- 1 tsp grated fresh ginger
- 1 cup plain nuts, finely chopped

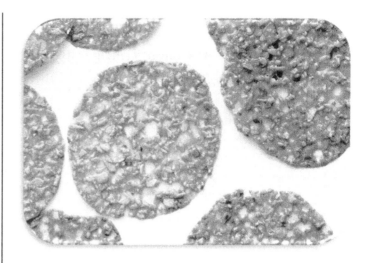

Instructions:

1. Preheat oven to 375°F.
2. Line thick aluminum cookie sheet with parchment paper because you want these cookies to spread very thin.
3. Grease parchment paper.
4. Combine brown sugar, butter, and corn syrup in a pan. Bring to a boil on top of stove.
5. Blend tapioca flour, arrowroot, and xanthan gum in a bowl.
6. Add the tapioca mixture to the sugar-and-butter mixture; blend well.
7. Add ginger and nuts.
8. Drop dough by the ½ tsp ful 2 inches apart on cookie sheet to allow space for the cookies to spread.
9. Bake for 5-6 minutes.
10. Let cookies harden on parchment paper-covered cookie sheets.
11. Turn cookie-laden parchment paper over onto cookie plate. Peel paper from cookies and arrange on plate.

Marshmallow Fluff Squares

Prep time: 25 minutes (+2 hours refrigerate)

Cooking time: 0 minutes

Servings: 20

Nutrients per serving:

Carbohydrates – 7.7 g

Fat – 1 g

Protein – 1 g

Calories – 34

Ingredients:

- 1 package GF butterscotch or GF chocolate chips
- ½ cup GF marshmallow fluff
- 3 cups GF puffed rice cereal

Instructions:

1. Grease a 9 x 13-inch baking pan and line with waxed paper.
2. Melt chips and marshmallow fluff over hot water in double boiler.
3. Remove from heat, add cereal, and combine.
4. Use greased hands to pat mixture into prepared baking pan.
5. Refrigerate for 2 hours, then cut into squares.

CAKES

Trampoline Cake

Prep time: 25 minutes

Cooking time: 1 hour

Servings: 12

Nutrients per serving:

Carbohydrates – 25.2 g

Fat – 1.7 g

Protein – 2.4 g

Calories – 126

Ingredients:

- 7 medium eggs, separated, at room temperature (70°F)
- ½ cup orange juice
- 1 tsp vanilla flavoring or extract
- ½ tsp cream of tartar
- 1½ cups sugar
- ½ cup rice flour
- ½ cup tapioca flour
- 1 tsp baking powder
- 1 tsp xanthan gum
- 1½ tsp salt

Instructions:

1. Grease a 9-inch tube pan or an 11 x 7-inch cake pan; sprinkle with rice flour.
2. Beat egg whites until foamy but not overly stiff.
3. Fold in cream of tartar to beaten whites.
4. Beat egg yolks in separate bowl.
5. Whisk yolks and sugar together until they form a "ribbon" as the mixture flows off the whisk.
6. Whisk orange juice and vanilla gradually into beaten yolks.
7. Add flours, baking powder, xanthan gum, and salt to yolk mixture. Blend.
8. Fold beaten egg whites into yolks.
9. Bake at 325°F for 30 minutes.
10. Reset oven temperature to 350°F. Bake for 30 minutes longer.

Zucchini Cake

Prep time: 15 minutes

Cooking time: 60 minutes

Servings: 20

Nutrients per serving:

Carbohydrates – 31.1 g

Fat – 43.4 g

Protein – 18.2 g

Calories – 588

Ingredients:

- 6 cups almond meal flour
- 4 tsp cinnamon
- 1 tsp baking soda
- 2 tsp baking powder
- ½ cup plain nuts, chopped
- 3 tsp xanthan gum
- ½ tsp sea salt
- 5 cups grated peeled zucchini (about 6 medium zucchini)
- ½ cup ripe bananas
- 6 eggs, well beaten
- ½ cup butter, melted
- ½ cup honey
- 2 tsp vanilla flavoring or extract

Instructions:

1. Preheat oven to 325°F.
2. Grease two 9-inch round cake pans and coat with flour. This can also be made in one 9-inch tube pan or a 9 x 5 x 3-inch loaf pan. Or, line two 12-cup muffin tins with paper liners and spray with oil spray.
3. Blend dry ingredients together so baking soda, baking powder, and xanthan gum are evenly distributed.
4. Mix all the wet ingredients together and then blend the wet into the dry—it makes a spongy mass, but don't worry.
5. Spoon batter into prepared cake pans.
6. Bake 45 to 60 minutes.
7. Cool on rack.

Tapioca White Cake

Prep time: 15 minutes

Cooking time: 40 minutes

Servings: 12

Nutrients per serving:

Carbohydrates – 24.9 g

Fat – 20.7 g

Protein – 3.9 g

Calories – 301

Ingredients:

- 4 eggs, separated and beaten
- 1 cup butter
- 2 tsp almond flavoring or extract
- ½ tsp cream of tartar
- ½ cup sugar
- 2 tsp vanilla flavoring or extract
- 1 cup tapioca flour
- ½ cup almond flour
- ½ tsp baking powder
- ½ tsp baking soda
- 1 tsp xanthan gum

Instructions:

1. Preheat oven to 350°F.
2. Grease 9-inch tube pan and dust with tapioca flour.
3. Beat egg whites in a clean bowl until stiff, and gradually add cream of tartar.
4. Cream butter and sugar in a separate bowl.
5. Add vanilla, beaten egg yolks, and almond flavoring to the butter mixture.
6. Combine flours, baking powder, baking soda, and xanthan gum.
7. Add flour mixture to butter mixture and stir well.
8. Fold in egg whites.
9. Bake for 35-40 minutes or till done.
10. Invert pan on top of rack. Place a wet towel on pan bottom to help loosen the cake. Tap pan to loosen. Carefully nudge it out.
11. Cool cake upside down on a rack. Invert onto plate when cool.

Nut and Buckwheat Spice Cake

Prep time: 15 minutes

Cooking time: 35 minutes

Servings: 12

Nutrients per serving:

Carbohydrates – 56.4 g

Fat – 30.3 g

Protein – 6.5 g

Calories – 527

Ingredients:

- 1 cup buckwheat flour
- ½ cup bean flour
- ½ cup hazelnut flour
- ½ tsp xanthan gum
- 1 tsp baking powder
- ½ tsp baking soda
- 3 Tbsp ground cinnamon
- 2 Tbsp cumin
- 1 tsp sea salt
- 1 cup plain chopped nuts (pecans or walnuts)
- 2 eggs
- 1 cup safflower oil or 1 cup unsalted butter, melted
- 1 cup honey
- 2 cups applesauce

Instructions:

1. Preheat oven to 350°F.
2. Lightly grease two 8-inch round cake pans or one 11 x 7-inch cake pan.
3. Mix dry ingredients, except nuts, together.
4. Beat eggs until fluffy.
5. Combine the oil or butter and honey; add to the beaten eggs.
6. Add dry ingredients to wet ingredients (except applesauce). Beat just until smooth.
7. Mix in applesauce and nuts.
8. Pour cake mixture into baking pan or pans.
9. Bake for approximately 25 minutes (2 round pans for layer cake) or 35 minutes (single rectangular cake pan). Test with toothpick for doneness.

Teff Gingerbread

Prep time: 15 minutes

Cooking time: 30 minutes

Servings: 16

Nutrients per serving:

Carbohydrates – 15.7 g

Fat – 30.3 g

Protein – 2.2 g

Calories – 106

Ingredients:

- 1½ cups teff flour
- ½ cup quinoa flour
- ½ cup buckwheat flour
- 1 tsp baking powder
- ½ tsp baking soda
- 2 tsp xanthan gum
- ½ cup light brown sugar, packed, or granulated maple sugar
- 2 tsp cinnamon
- 2 tsp ground ginger or 3 tsp grated fresh ginger
- ½ tsp sea salt
- 1 tsp grated nutmeg
- ½ tsp allspice
- ½ tsp ground cloves
- 1 egg
- 4 Tbsp butter, melted
- 1 cup buttermilk
- ¼ cup unsulfured molasses (optional)

Instructions:

1. Preheat oven 425°F.
2. Grease a 9-inch square cake pan; dust with rice flour.
3. Blend dry ingredients in bowl.
4. Blend wet ingredients in another bowl.
5. Whisk wet ingredients into dry.
6. Bake for 30 minutes, or until toothpick inserted in center comes out dry.

Banana Cake

Prep time: 15 minutes

Cooking time: 40 minutes

Servings: 16

Nutrients per serving:

Carbohydrates – 35 g

Fat – 15.4 g

Protein – 8.4 g

Calories – 312

Ingredients:

- 1½ cups almond meal flour
- 1½ cups amaranth or sorghum flour
- ½ cup arrowroot
- ½ tsp sea salt
- 1 tsp baking powder
- 1 tsp baking soda
- 1 tsp xanthan gum
- 3 ripe bananas, mashed
- 2 Tbsp lemon juice
- ½ cup butter, melted
- ½ cup honey
- 3 eggs
- 2 tsp vanilla flavoring or extract

Instructions:

1. Preheat oven to 350°F.
2. Grease 9-inch square pan; dust with rice flour.
3. Blend all dry ingredients in large mixing bowl.
4. Blend wet ingredients in a separate bowl using electric mixer.
5. Pour liquid ingredients over dry and stir gently.
6. Pour into baking dish.
7. Bake for 40 minutes; test with toothpick for doneness.

Cranberry Loaf Cake

Prep time: 15 minutes

Cooking time: 40 minutes

Servings: 12

Nutrients per serving:

Carbohydrates – 43 g

Fat – 14.6 g

Protein – 7.9 g

Calories – 336

Ingredients:

- ½ cup rice flour
- 1 cup almond meal flour
- ½ cup hazelnut flour
- 2 tsp nutmeg
- 1 tsp cumin
- 1½ tsp baking soda
- 1 cup GF dried cranberries
- 2 eggs, beaten till frothy
- 1 Tbsp oil
- 1 cup plain yogurt
- ½ cup GF rice syrup
- ½ cup orange juice
- ½ cup jam, marmalade, or conserves (apricot, strawberry, pineapple, etc.)

Instructions:

1. Preheat oven to 350°F.
2. Grease one 8 x 4 x 3-inch loaf pan.
3. Mix dry ingredients (except fruit) together.
4. Mix wet ingredients (except jam, marmalade, or conserves) together.
5. Combine wet and dry ingredients. (Add a few more drops of juice or water if mixture is dry.)
6. Fold dried fruit and preserves into batter.
7. Bake in prepared loaf pan for 40 minutes or until top is golden.

Chocolate Dump-It Cake

Prep time: 15 minutes

Cooking time: 25 minutes

Servings: 18

Nutrients per serving:

Carbohydrates – 31.6 g

Fat – 4.5 g

Protein – 1.7 g

Calories – 174

Ingredients:

- ½ cup pure GF cocoa powder
- ½ cup boiling water
- 1 cup cornstarch
- 1½ cups potato starch
- 1 Tbsp plus 1½ tsp baking powder
- 1 tsp salt
- 1 cup sugar
- 1 can of cherry pie filling
- 2 eggs, beaten until frothy
- ½ cup canola oil
- 2 tsp vanilla flavoring or extract
- 2½ tsp guar gum or xanthan gum
- 1¼ cups milk, divided

Instructions:

1. Preheat oven to 350°F.
2. Grease a 9 x 13- inch pan.
3. Combine cocoa powder and boiling water in a large bowl; mix well.
4. Add remaining ingredients, except for 1 cup milk. Mix well to remove all lumps from batter.
5. Add milk slowly. Mix just until combined. Add a little more milk if batter seems heavy.
6. Pour batter into prepared pan.
7. Bake for 22-25 minutes, until a toothpick inserted in the middle of the cake tests clean.

Carob Fudge Cake

Prep time: 15 minutes

Cooking time: 30 minutes

Servings: 12

Nutrients per serving:

Carbohydrates – 34.9 g

Fat – 8.6 g

Protein – 3.4 g

Calories – 231

Ingredients:

- 1 cup brown rice flour, sifted
- ½ cup amaranth flour, sifted
- ½ cup pure carob powder
- 1 tsp baking soda
- ½ tsp sea salt
- ½ cup plain nuts, chopped
- ½ cup warm water
- ½ cup oil
- ½ cup honey
- 1 Tbsp vinegar or lemon juice
- 1 tsp vanilla flavoring or extract

Instructions:

1. Preheat oven to 350°F.
2. Grease 8-inch square baking pan; set aside.
3. Combine dry ingredients, except nuts, in a bowl. Mix well, then sift into another bowl.
4. Combine wet ingredients in a small bowl. Mix together with fork or whisk.
5. Pour mixed wet ingredients over dry ingredients (all at once), then mix quickly.
6. Pour immediately into prepared baking pan. Scatter nuts on top of batter.
7. Bake 25 to 30 minutes. When done, cracks will (typically) appear in top. The inside remains moist and fudgy.

Carrot Cake

Prep time: 15 minutes

Cooking time: 50 minutes

Servings: 10

Nutrients per serving:

Carbohydrates – 68.9 g

Fat – 27.9 g

Protein – 9.6 g

Calories – 565

Ingredients:

- 1½ cups teff flour
- 1 cup tapioca flour
- ½ cup fava bean flour
- 2 tsp xanthan gum
- 1 tsp baking soda
- 2 tsp cinnamon
- 2 tsp ground ginger
- 3 cups shredded carrots
- 1 cup plain pecans, chopped
- ½ cup butter, softened
- 1 cup brown sugar, packed, or 1 cup honey
- 4 eggs, at room temperature, beaten
- 1 cup plain yogurt
- 1 tsp vanilla flavoring or extract
- 1 cup crushed pineapple

Icing:

- 3 ounces GF cream cheese, softened
- 2 cups GF confectioners' sugar
- 2 Tbsp milk
- 1 tsp almond flavoring or extract

Instructions:

1. Preheat oven to 350°F.
2. Grease a 9-inch springform or tube pan; dust with rice flour.
3. Combine flours, xanthan gum, baking powder, baking soda, cinnamon, and ginger together in bowl.
4. Cream together butter and sugar in a large bowl.
5. Whisk in eggs.
6. Add yogurt and vanilla, blend.
7. Add flour mixture to the egg mixture; stir just until blended.
8. Stir in carrots, pecans, and pineapple.
9. Pour batter into prepared pan.
10. Bake 45-50 minutes, until toothpick inserted in center comes out clean.

Hazelnut Applesauce Cake

Prep time: 20 minutes

Cooking time: 40 minutes

Servings: 12

Nutrients per serving:

Carbohydrates – 33.1 g

Fat – 19.1 g

Protein – 3.8 g

Calories – 319

Ingredients:

- 1½ cups hazelnut flour
- 1 cup currants or other GF dried fruit
- ½ cup plain pecans, chopped
- ½ cup bean flour
- ½ cup tapioca flour
- ½ tsp baking soda
- ½ tsp baking powder
- ½ tsp cream of tartar
- ½ tsp salt
- 1 tsp ground cloves
- 1 tsp xanthan gum
- ½ cup unsalted butter, melted
- ½ cup maple syrup
- 1 large egg, beaten
- 2 cups applesauce

Instructions:

1. Preheat oven to 350°F.
2. Grease an 8-inch square cake pan and dust lightly with rice or quinoa flour.
3. Sprinkle some of the hazelnut flour over the fruit and nuts in separate bowl; toss until coated.
4. Blend remaining hazelnut flour with dry ingredients (except fruit and nuts).
5. Combine wet ingredients; mix well.
6. Mix wet ingredients into dry ingredients, blending well.
7. Fold nuts and fruit into the batter.
8. Spoon or pour batter into prepared cake pan.
9. Bake for 40 minutes or until toothpick comes out clean.

CONCLUSION

Thank you for reading this book and having the patience to try the recipes.

I do hope that you have had as much enjoyment reading and experimenting with the meals as I have had writing the book.

If you would like to leave a comment, you can do so at the Order section->Digital orders, in your Amazon account.

Stay safe and healthy!

Recipe Index

Conversion Tables

VOLUME EQUIVALENTS (LIQUID)

US STANDARD	US STANDARD (OUNCES)	METRIC
2 tablespoons	1 fl. oz.	30 mL
1/4 cup	2 fl. oz.	60 mL
1/2 cup	4 fl. oz.	120 mL
1 cup	8 fl. oz.	240mL
1 1/2 cups	12 fl. oz.	355 mL
2 cups or 1 pint	16 fl. oz.	475 mL
4 cups or 1 quart	32 fl. oz.	1 L
1 gallon	128 fl. oz.	4 L

OVEN TEMPERATURES

FAHRENHEIT (°F)	CELSIUS (°C) APPROXIMATE
250 °F	120 °C
300 °F	150 °C
325 °F	165 °C
350 °F	180 °C
375 °F	190 °C
400 °F	200 °C
425 °F	220 °C
450 °F	230 °C

VOLUME EQUIVALENTS (LIQUID)

US STANDARD	METRIC (APPROXIMATE)
1/8 teaspoon	0.5 mL
1/4 teaspoon	1 mL
1/2 teaspoon	2 mL
2/3 teaspoon	4 mL
1 teaspoon	5 mL
1 tablespoon	15 mL
1/4 cup	59 mL
1/3 cup	79 mL
1/2 cup	118 mL
2/3 cup	156 mL
3/4 cup	177 mL
1 cup	235 mL
2 cups or 1 pint	475 mL
3 cups	700 mL
4 cups or 1 quart	1 L
1/2 gallon	2 L
1 gallon	4 L

WEIGHT EQUIVALENTS

US STANDARD	METRIC (APPROXIMATE)
1/2 ounce	15 g
1 ounce	30 g
2 ounces	60 g
4 ounces	115 g
8 ounces	225 g
12 ounces	340 g
16 ounces or 1 pound	455 g

Other Books by Tiffany Shelton

Tiffany Shelton's page on Amazon

https://goo.gl/4cpNvM

Made in the USA
Coppell, TX
17 November 2019

11479289R00044